ERO SERIES VOL. 24

# BOEING B-52

## "Stratofortress"

*by*

### WILLIAM G. HOLDER

ISBN-0-8168-0590-3

**AERO PUBLISHERS, INC.**
*329 West Aviation Road, Fallbrook, CA 92028*

# DEDICATION

To my Mother-In-Law, Mrs. L. C. Shenberger, who has been one of my biggest boosters during my writing career.

# ACKNOWLEDGEMENTS

The author wishes to thank the following individuals and organizations for their unselfish assistance during the preparation of this document.

USAF Office of Information, ASD 0I/Mr. Maltby
AFSC Office of Information
The Research Staff of the Air Force Museum
AFLC Office of Information/Lt. Col. Nick Apple
AFLC Historical Archives
Boeing Company/Wichita Division/ Jack Wecker-News Bureau Dir.
17th Bomb Wing(SAC)
Major Buzz Chamblee-17th Bomb Wing
Office of Information-Edwards Air Force Base
Hq. SAC, Office of Information
Office of Information, Davis-Monthan Air Force Base
Pratt and Whitney Aircraft, Public Relations Department
Public Relations Department, McDonnell-Douglas Corp.
Mr. Dale Witt-Photography
Mrs. Phyllis Ann Trimble-Typing
Frank Stallman-Artwork
Lt. Col. Jenson-SAF0I

Library of Congress Cataloging in Publication Data

Holder, William G        1937-
   Boeing B-52 "Stratofortress"

(Aero series ; v. 24)
  1. B-52 Bomber. I. Title.
UG1242.B6H64        358.4'2        75-7464
ISBN 0-8168-0588-1

# TABLE OF CONTENTS

Something big was in the air! The busy flight ramp t Anderson Air Force Base in Guam was abuzz. Maintenance crews sweated over their giant B-52's, hecking every nut and bolt. Bombs were loaded in-rnally into the Stratoforts' massive bomb bays on reloaded bomb racks. Twenty-four bombs on the xternal wing racks were hung one at a time. It was ecember 1972, and the B-52 was going to face its oughest challenge ever—"LINEBACKER II" was on!

The flight crews heard the news three hours before ke-off on that first day. " . . . Gentlemen, we are oing to strike targets in the Hanoi-Haiphong area . . " Weather: " . . . It's bad . . . " Enemy Defenses: ". . Tough." Order of battle: " . . . Max effort." The B-2's had for years, basically unmolested, been aturation bombing in South Vietnam, but this would e the first maximum effort "Up North." The crews new it would be tough going.

The B-52's pounded North Vietnam for eleven days during which time more than 1,000 SAM's were launched against the fleet. Many times the missiles came up in salvos of two and four. And when the SAM's got through, the MiG's were waiting. For those bloody and heroic eleven days the skies over North Vietnam were alive with bursting SAM's, flashing rockets and falling, burning airplanes . . . A goodly number of which were the giant B-52 Stratoforts.

The losses of LINEBACKER II were high . . . Many felt that they were too high. Some 26 aircraft were lost of which 15 were B-52's. Actually the loss amounted to two percent of the B-52's involved. During the operation the B-52's flew a total of some 700 sorties.

But the giant Stratoforts did the job! And with the termination of LINEBACKER II, the SEA conflict

*The roll-out of the XB-52 one rainy night in Seattle was shrouded in secrecy as evidenced by the tarp which completely covered the aircraft.*
*(Boeing Photo)*

The XB-52 and the B-36 in the background at Lackland, far on the right, is the original XB-52.

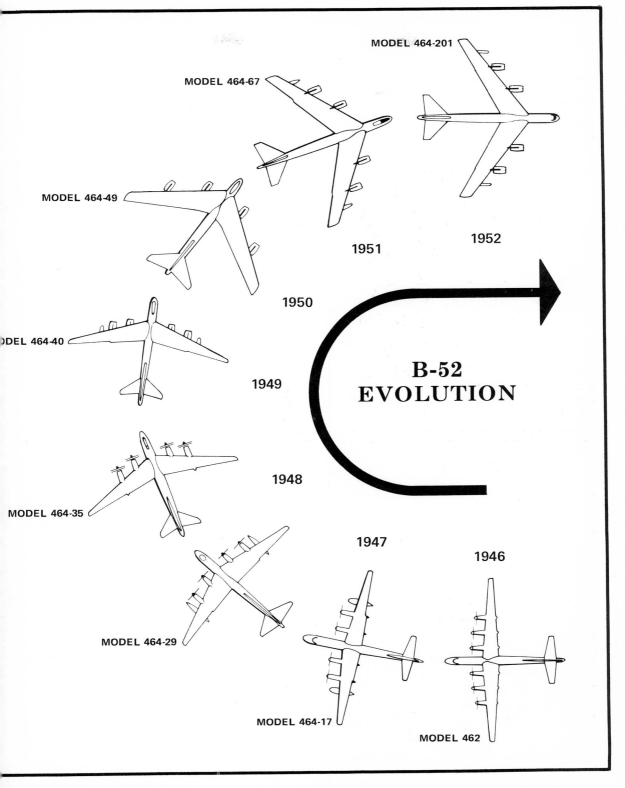

MODEL 464-201

MODEL 464-67

MODEL 464-49

1951

1952

1950

MODEL 464-40

1949

B-52
EVOLUTION

1948

MODEL 464-35

1947

1946

MODEL 464-29

MODEL 464-17

MODEL 462

*The evolution of the B-52 showed a start with a six-engine straight wing design and culmination with the known B-52 design of today.*
*(Artwork by Frank Stallman)*

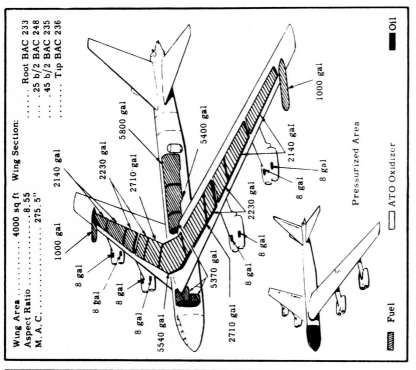

Wing Area ............ 4000 sq ft   Wing Section:
Aspect Ratio .......... 8.55        ..... Root BAC 233
M. A. C. ............. 275.5"       ..... .25 b/2 BAC 248
                                    ..... .45 b/2 BAC 235
                                    ..... Tip BAC 236

1000 gal
2140 gal
2230 gal
2710 gal
5800 gal
5400 gal
2140 gal
8 gal
8 gal
1000 gal
8 gal
8 gal
8 gal
8 gal
2230 gal
8 gal
8 gal
5370 gal
5540 gal
2710 gal

Pressurized Area

▨ Fuel      □ ATO Oxidizer      ■ Oil

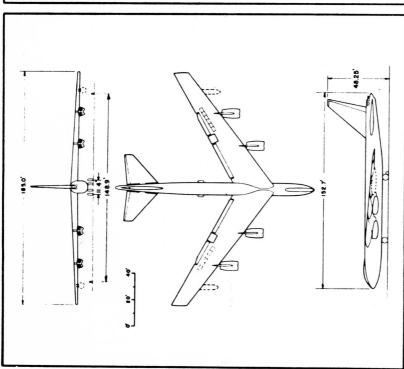

185.0'
11.4'
148.9'
152.7'
48.25'
0   40'   80'

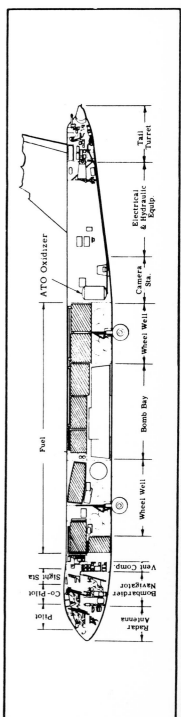

Tail Turret
Electrical & Hydraulic Equip.
Camera Sta.
Wheel Well
Bomb Bay
Wheel Well
Vent. Comp.
Sight Sta
Navigator
Bombardier
Co-Pilot
Pilot
Radar Antenna
ATO Oxidizer
Fuel

*Black rubber smears mark the runway after a landing of the XB-52 during a flight test. (USAF Photo)*

*The clean flowing lines of the Stratofortress are vividly illustrated by this head-on shot of the XB-52*

*The Boeing B-47 shown taking off with JATO bottles. This aircraft had a great influence on some of the features of the B-52.*
*(USAF Photo)*

ground to a stand-down. The B-52 had proven in Vietnam, what the B-17 and B-29 had in World War II—that is, the total devastation of the enemy homeland with conventional ordnance can be the winning hand for stopping of hostilities. The giant B-52 with 108 "Iron Bombs" was indeed a devastating weapon. But the bird was, in effect, playing a role for which she had never been cast. Conceived in the time of nuclear weapon infancy and the climate of the "Cold War," the B-52 had been envisioned as a high-altitude carrier of nuclear destruction. Its conversion to an iron bomb hauler is but one of the many transitions this amazing and versatile aircraft has seen during its lifetime . . .

The B-52's genealogical roots go deep. As early as 1945, the Army Air Force discussed the possibilities and characteristics for new post-war bombers. By November of that year, definite characteristics for a high-speed, high-altitude, long range bomber had been formulated. The requirements called for a plane capable of "carrying ten thousand pounds of bombs for 5,000 miles while operating at a speed of 300 mph at 35,000 feet."

There were proposals for the new aircraft submitted by Martin, Consolidated Vultee and Boeing. The Consolidated Vultee entry would evolve into the XB-60 bomber which was basically a swept-wing, jet powered version of its B-36.

Boeing submitted a design, Model 462, for a six-engined design weighing 360,000 pounds with a 3,110-mile radius and a 410 mph cruising speed. The straight-wing design, which bore a marked similarity to the previous B-29, featured a nose-wheel undercarriage arrangement which retracted into the engine nacelle. However, the Air Materiel Command was greatly concerned about the model's extremely high gross weight which caused alternate configurations to be examined.

During discussions of new medium bombers, Boeing presented Design Study 464 which outlined a four-engine aircraft with a gross weight of 230,000 pounds and a 400 mph cruising speed. In 1946, plans were formulated for a four-engine aircraft capable of carrying nuclear weapons, a 12,000 mile range and a 400 mph cruising speed. Studies by Boeing resulted in two designs differing only in bomb load capabilities. The Model 464-16 carried only 10,000 pounds whereas the general-purpose 464-17 Model had a bomb bay capacity of 90,000 pounds. Work was started on the -17 design but was halted in June 1947, when new heavy bomber requirements were formulated.

With the mastering of in-flight refueling being developed, the planners' attentions then turned to an aircraft with greater speed capability. An improved model evolved from Boeing drawing boards as the Model 464-29 and featured a 20 degree sweep in the wings along with a more sharply tapered wing. Grossing out at about 400,000 pounds, Boeing engineers calculated a maximum

*The YB-52 in one of its early test flights. Although this aircraft was built later than the XB-52, it flew first.* *(Boeing Photo)*

speed of almost 450 mph. Several other turbo-prop models were considered including the Model 464-35 which promised a top speed of 500 mph. For almost three years the XB-52 bomber had floundered through a series of changing requirements and revisions. The airplane, during that time period, for the most part had resembled the B-17, B-29, and B-50 forerunners. The B-52 had been designed to replace the B-36 yet the turbo-prop propulsion of the initial designs provided only minimal advantages over the Consolidated Vultee aircraft.

In May 1948, Boeing was asked to expand their performance studies and include configuration studies using pure jet power. It was obvious to the engineers that with the improving jet engine technology, pure jet power was the only way to go.

The high speed and comparative simplicity of the pure jet engine was quickly being established. Experimental flights of the pure-jet B-47 were proving highly successful. The troublesome fuel consumption aspects of the jet engine had been solved.

So it was not surprising that the 464-40 Model was born incorporating jet power—namely, Westinghouse J-40 jet engines. The jet version incorporated a minimum of changes from the turbo-prop version with no increase in the lift-off weight. Models 464-46 and -47 were further refinements of the -40 design with consideration on using the new P & W J57 engine.

With the advent of Model 464-49, the Boeing engineers had come up with an aircraft that was finally starting to look like the B-52 does today. (But in other respects it also looked a lot like a scaled-up B-47 also under advanced development during this time period.) The new design incorporated eight J57 turbo-jets, possessed additional fuel capacity and carried only one turret instead of the previous two. However, the new bird did show a 50,000 pound increase in gross weight. But it didn't take the Air Force long to decide that this was indeed the aircraft it had been looking for. The XB-52 would be an eight-jet, swept wing creation.

From a performance standpoint, the 464-49 possessed some outstanding characteristics. It was to have a design gross weight of 330,000 pounds, a range of 8,000 miles and a top speed of 572 miles per hour. The bombing altitude was assessed as 45,000 feet.

During the evolutionary process to the -49 Model and the slightly refined Model 464-201, upon which the XB-52 prototype was constructed, major problems faced the development. It was time for the jet age but the old prop-powered, straight-wing school still had deep roots and rejected change. Weight-adding armament, and how much to have presented many arguments. Heavy landing gears also added greatly to weight problems. It was even considered for a time to drop certain outboard lan

12

ding gear components after take-off to lighten the gross weight. Crew size arguments raged with some configurations having as many as 15 on station.

The five or so years of B-52 definition had seen a tremendous evolutionary process take place. In fact, it could well be defined as a move from the straight-wing technology of WWII to the swept-wing jet era. Through the evolutionary process the gross weight remained nearly constant at about 400,000 pounds, but the speed capability increased from 382 knots (Model 462) to 490 knots on the final configuration.

The time for metal cutting had finally arrived. There would be two prototypes—coined the XB-52 and the YB-52. The XB-52 was the first. Grossing out at some 390,000 pounds, the XB-52 in many ways resembled a scaled-up B-47. The XB-52 sported a 35 degree sweep and eight (two per pod) J57 turbojets. The aircraft also demonstrated two four-wheel, fuselage-mounted bogeys which possessed a unique cross-wind capability. Wing-tip mounted wheels were required because of wing-droop with a full fuel load. The XB-52 also carried a large braking parachute in the tail compartment.

The Air Force knew it really had something with its new super bomber and a tight cloak of secrecy covered its development. Early photographs showed the new aircraft covered with concealing tarps much like the new model year cars used to use. Extensive modifications had to be made on the XB-52 before it was ready for flight which did not occur till October 2, 1952. This delay allowed the second prototype, the so-called YB-52 to make the first flights. On September 4, 1954, the YB-52 made a Seattle-to-Dayton run at a speed of 624 miles per hour, better than the time made by jet fighters in the Bendix Trophy Race from California to Dayton.

The B-47 influence was also evident on the XB-52 (and also the YB-52) with the tandem seating arrangement for the pilot and co-pilot. This situation, however, would be altered for production Stratoforts which would have side-by-side seating.

The B-52 flight tests with the X and Y prototypes proved that the Stratofort was ready. It was time to get the production lines rolling!

*The YB-52 in a test flight. The tandem seating arrangement for the pilot and co-pilot can be clearly seen. This concept would be abandoned later in the B-52A for side-by-side seating. (USAF Photo)*

*The immense size of the new aircraft is vividly realized in this picture where the YB-52 is alongside a*

# Chapter II
# Models and Mods

For some eleven years the B-52 production lines hummed. In all, some 742 Stratofortresses were produced of which some 275 were built at the Boeing Seattle facility. But the bulk of the production program, including all of the later models, were produced at the giant Boeing Wichita Plant, some 467 in all.

In all, some seven major different models evolved from the Boeing drawing boards. And it can be definitely stated that the B-52 program started on sounder footing than any other large aircraft program. In fact, the Air Force authorized production tooling contracts ahead of actual production contracts. Only once in U.S. aviation history had similar confidence been shown in a new airplane before the first flight—the B-29.

## MODELS

The B-52A, of which there were three constructed, maintained a basic similarity to the previous YB and XB prototypes. The basic difference evolved from the addition of a four-feet lengthened nose contour, and elimination of the B-47-type bubble canopy. Carrying a crew of six, the A configurations were equipped with J57-P-9W powerplants and grossed out at about 390,000 pounds. Carrying two 1,000 pound drop tanks, the B-52A could turn 490 knots at over 46,000 feet.

The initial B-52A rolled out of the Seattle plant on March 18, 1954, and made its first flight test on August 5, 1954. These first three A-Model Stratoforts would never see operational SAC service and would later serve basic test functions. (See Chapter 3)

On January 25, 1955, the first B-52B took to the air from Seattle. The B-Model would be the first Stratofort to be delivered to SAC—namely the 93rd Bomb Wing. The B variant incorporated several changes including the MA-6A bombing navigation system. RB-52B was the designation given to some 52B's which incorporated a reconnaissance capability. Twenty-seven were built. The B-52B was the version which set the first of many significant B-52

The first Stratofortress, the B-52A—Serial Number 2001. The A Models never entered SAC service.
(Boeing Photo)

15

B-52B, Serial Number 2012, was one of the first of the B Models to be produced. The B looked quite

Brand spanking new B-52B's sit on the Boeing flight line in Seattle. These particular aircraft were delivered to the Air Force in 1954 and 1955.
(Boeing Photo)

*The RB-52B is shown being checked out at Wright Patterson Air Force Base. (Air Force Museum Pho*

*Picture of the Air Force Museum's B-52B. The aircraft is on permanent display in the outside exhibit area. Another can be seen at the SAC Museum at Offutt Air Force Base, Nebraska.*

*(Photo by author)*

*One of the many Stratoforts at Davis-Monthan Air Force Base, this B-52B awaits her fate.* (AF Museum Photo)

This brand-new B-52C is shown during flight "at altitude." The wing-tip

First released photo of the B-52C.   (USAF Photo)

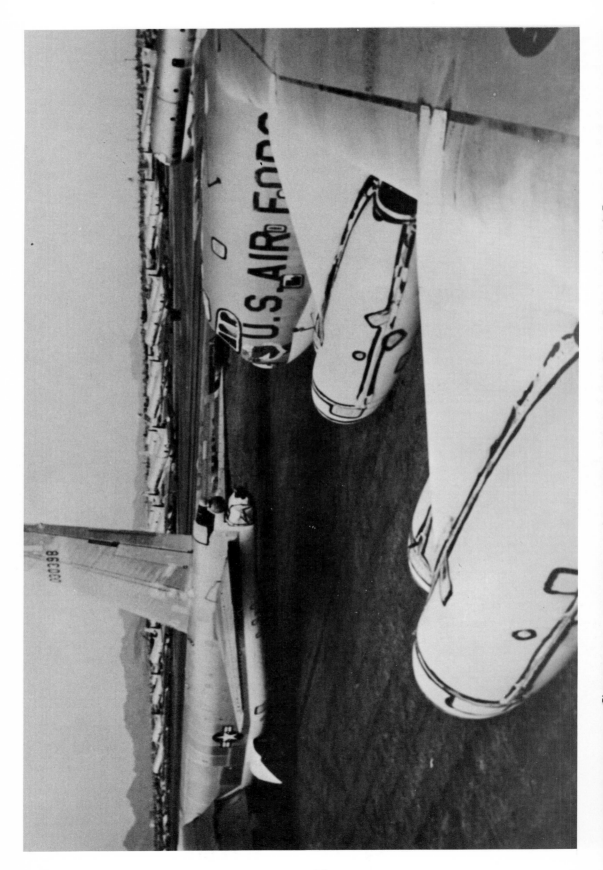

range and endurance records. Three B-52B's, flying at an average speed of 452 knots, turned a round-the-world trip on January 18, 1957, in 45 hours, 19 minutes.

March 9, 1956, saw the first flight of the B-52C—the last pure Seattle-produced Stratofort. The B-52C incorporated larger underwing drop tanks and had its all-up weight increased to 450,000 pounds. Actually the B-52C was a product of the evolutionary process and could have been called essentially and improved B-52B. Thirty-five were constructed.

With the advent of the D Model, the B-52 also began production at Wichita although of the 170 B-52D's that were produced, 101 were built at Seattle. The Seattle Stratoforts were built concurrently with the KC-135A tanker-transports. With the exception of the later G and H Models, the D Model was the most multiple model built. The first B-52D test flight occurred at Seattle on September 28, 1956. During its lifetime the B-52D would see a significant modification for Vietnam operations.

Exactly 100 B-52E aircraft were built with Wichita assuming production leadership with 58 produced. The first B-52E flight took place at Seattle on October 3, 1957, with the Wichita flight taking place some two weeks later. The B-52E was the first B-52 to carry the Hound-Dog missile along with incorporating improved bombing, navigation and electronics systems.

## B-52 PRODUCTION TOTALS

The Boeing Company's Wichita, Kansas, facilities produced 467 B-52's for the Strategic Air Command, while Seattle was responsible for the manufacture of 275, plus one each XB-52 and YB-52.

A total of 742 B-52's had been produced by Wichita and Seattle when the program ended September 1962.

| Models | Seattle | Wichita | Totals |
|--------|---------|---------|--------|
| B-52A | 3 | — | 3 |
| B-52B | 50 | — | 50 |
| B-52C | 35 | — | 35 |
| B-52D | 101 | 69 | 170 |
| B-52E | 42 | 58 | 100 |
| B-52F | 44 | 45 | 89 |
| B-52G | — | 193 | 193 |
| B-52H | — | 102 | 102 |
| Totals | 275 | 467 | 742 |

B-52 Deliveries by Years (Production)

| | Wichita | Seattle | Total |
|--------|---------|---------|-------|
| 1954 | 0 | 5 | 5 |
| 1955 | 0 | 34 | 34 |
| 1956 | 10 | 65 | 75 |
| 1957 | 78 | 96 | 174 |
| 1958 | 91 | 65 | 156 |
| 1959 | 108 | 10 | 118 |
| 1960 | 73 | 0 | 73 |
| 1961 | 62 | 0 | 62 |
| 1962 | 45 | 0 | 45 |
| | 467 | 275 | 742 |

*The details of this Wichita-built B-52E spill over the landscape. Giant flaps are fully deployed. The immense size of the aircraft can be gauged from the size of the maintenance personnel at the tail of the aircraft.*
(USAF Photo)

An underside view of the B-52F. The picture clearly shows the landing configuration with the Fowler

*A wichita-built B-52F awaits its ultimate fate in storage at Davis-Monthan Air Force Base. The desert conditions at this Arizona facility allow the storage of aircraft for long periods of time with little deterioration.* (USAF Photo)

Many improvements were incorporated into the B-52G. Model was easily recognized by the

*The long sweeping wing of the B-52H is vividly illustrated by this picture. The H Model identification can be made from the two-step diameter appearance of the turbofan engines.   (Boeing Photo)*

*Low angle 3/4 rear view of a B-52H in flight trailing majestic contrails. (USAF Photo)*

*Sun rays tend to engulf the flowing lines of a B-52H. Exhaust smears can be clearly seen on the underside of the wings.*
*(USAF Photo)*

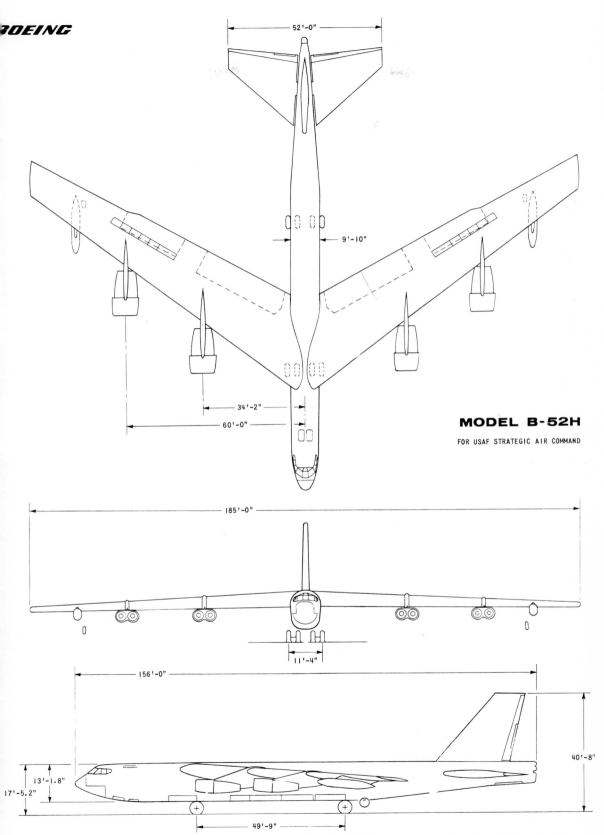

**MODEL B-52H**

FOR USAF STRATEGIC AIR COMMAND

52'-0"

9'-10"

34'-2"

60'-0"

185'-0"

11'-4"

156'-0"

40'-8"

13'-1.8"

17'-5.2"

49'-9"

*Three view drawing of the B-52H, the final result of the evolutionary process. The final Stratofort was far different than the B-52A that started the line.* (Boeing Photo)

# B-52 MAJOR MODEL DIFFERENCES

| MODEL | AF SERIAL NO. | A/P PROD. NO. | INITIAL DELIVERY | FIRE CONTROL SYSTEM | BOMB NAV. SYSTEM | ENGINES | EXTERNAL DROP TANKS GALS. | MAXIMUM GROSS WT. LBS. | OPERATING WT. EMPTY LBS. | FUEL CAPACITY |
|---|---|---|---|---|---|---|---|---|---|---|
| XB-52 | 49-230 | 1 (Prototype) | Apr. 1953 | None | None | 4 J57-P-38<br>2 J75 | 1000 | 405,000 | | 38,865 |
| YB-52 | 49-231 | 1 (Prototype) | Mar. 1953 | None | None | J57-P-3 | 1000 | 420,000 | 167,509 | 37,550 |
| B-52A | 52-001 thru 52-003 | 1-3 | Jun. 1954 | A-3A | None | J57-P-1W | 1000 | 420,000 | 167,509 | 37,550 |
| B-52B | 52-004 thru 52-013<br>52-8710 thru 52-8716<br>53-366 thru 53-376<br>53-377 thru 53-391 | 4-13<br>14-20<br>21-31<br>32-46 | Sep. 1954<br>Jun. 1955<br>Aug. 1955<br>Nov. 1955 | A-3A<br>MD-5<br>MD-5<br>MD-5 | MA-6A<br>MA-6A<br>MA-6A<br>MA-6A | J57-P-1W<br><br>J57-P-29W* or<br>J57-P-29WA or<br>J57-P-19W | 1000 | 420,000 | 169,599 | 37,550 |
| | 53-392 thru 53-398 | 47-53 | Feb. 1956 | A-3A | MA-6A | | | | | |
| B-52C | 53-399 thru 53-408<br>53-2664 thru 53-2688 | 54-63<br>64-88 | Apr. 1956<br>Jun. 1956 | A-3A | | J57-P-29WA or<br>J57-P-19W | 3000 | 450,000 | 170,745 | 41,550 |
| B-52D Seattle | 55-068 thru 55-117<br>56-580 thru 56-630 | 89-138<br>139-189 | Oct. 1956<br>Apr. 1957 | MD-9 | AN/ASQ-48(V)<br>AN/ASB-15<br>AN/APN-108<br>MD-1 | J57-P-29W* or<br>J57-P-19W | 3000 | 450,000 | 171,666 | 41,550 |
| B-52D Wichita | 55-049 thru 55-067<br>55-673 thru 55-680<br>56-657 thru 56-698 | 1-19<br>20-27<br>28-69 | Jun. 1956<br>Mar. 1957<br>Jun. 1957 | | | J57-P-19W | | | | |
| B-52E Seattle | 56-631 thru 56-656<br>57-014 thru 57-029 | 190-215<br>216-231 | Nov. 1957<br>Feb. 1958 | MD-9 | AN/ASQ-38(V)<br>AN/ASB-4A | J57-P-29W* or<br>J57-P-19W | 3000 | 450,000 | 172,602 | 41,550 |
| B-52E Wichita | 56-699 thru 56-712<br>57-095 thru 57-138 | 70-83<br>84-127 | Nov. 1957<br>Dec. 1957 | | AN/APN-89A<br>MD-1, AJA-1 | J57-P-19W | | | | |
| B-52F Seattle | 57-030 thru 57-073 | 232-275 | May 1958 | MD-9 | AN/ASQ-38(V)<br>AN/ASB-4A | J57-P-43W or<br>J57-P-43WA or<br>J57-P-43WB | 3000 | 450,000 | 170,228 | 41,550 |
| B-52F Wichita | 57-139 thru 57-183 | 128-172 | Jun. 1958 | | AN/APN-89A<br>MD-1, AJA-1 | | | | | |
| B-52G Wichita | 57-6468 thru 57-6520<br>58-158 thru 58-258<br>59-2564 thru 59-2602 | 173-225<br>226-326<br>327-365 | Oct. 1958<br>Jul. 1959<br>Jun. 1960 | AN/ASG-15 | AN/ASQ-38(V)<br>AN/ASB-16<br>AN/APN-89A<br>MD-1, AJA-1 | J57-P-43W or<br>J57-P-43WB | 700 (Fixed) | 488,000 | 164,091 | 47,975 (Integral Fuel Wing) |
| B-52H Wichita | 60-001 & On | 366 & On | Mar. 1961 | AN/ASG-21 | AN/ASQ-38(V)<br>AN/ASB-9A<br>AN/APN-89A<br>MD-1, AJN-8<br>J-4 | TF33-P-3 | 700 (Fixed) | 488,000 | 165,466 | 47,975 (Integral Fuel Wing) |

* -29W Engines have 1/2 Water Rate Capability. These engines to be modified to full capability.
-29WA & -29WB Engines have Full Water Rate Capability.

*The wing-joining operation for the B-52 is carried out with exacting carefulness. The strong carry-through structure must carry the weight of eight jet engines, external ordnance and in the later models large amounts of fuel carried in the wings.* (Boeing Photo)

*Dynamic testing being accomplished by Boeing to verify the structural stability of the Stratofortress. Over the years the B-52 has proved to be one of the most durable aircraft in USAF history. (Boeing Photo)*

*Large cranes lower a large portion of the B-52 fuselage down to floor level where it can be mated with the rear section. Bomb bay section of elevated section can be easily identified. (Boeing Photo)*

*Final assembly of a whole room of B-52's that are not far from rolling out the door. SAC emblem can already be seen adorning the nose sections. On the lower left of the photo can be clearly seen the refueling recepticle where the probe from KC-135's is inserted for mid-air refueling. (Boeing Photo)*

The last of the breed. Work is shown preparing a B-52H. The giant turbo-fan engines can be characterized by their two-step diameter. (Boeing Photo)

The last B-52H, and for that matter the last B-52, was rolled out from Boeing-Wichita on June 22,

*Largest structural program ever performed was accomplished at USAF's Oklahoma City Air Materiel Area. Modification consisted of massive skin replacement on the fuselage. (USAF Photo)*

*A B-52G undergoes vertical stabilizer modification at the Oklahoma City Air Materiel Area.(USAF Photo)*

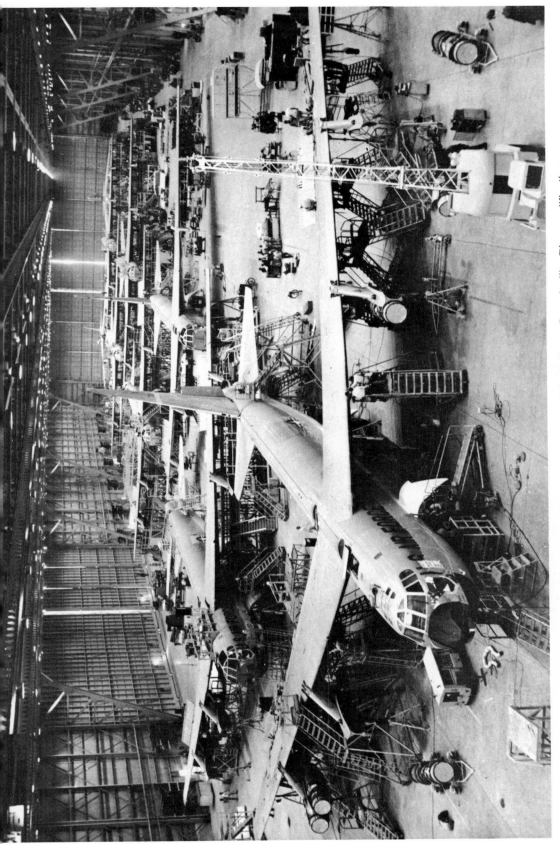

Another shot of the massive modification efforts at the Kelly Air Force Base facility. The modifications that have been performed by both Boeing and the Air Force have been responsible for greatly lengthening the career of the B-52.
(USAF Photo)

*Low Bridge!! Technicians at the Oklahoma modification facility work on the giant vertical fin of a B-*

The last Seattle-produced B-52 was the F Model ~ing Seattle a total Stratofort production output of ~e 275 aircraft. The B-52F incorporated so-called ~rd-drive" alternators which were connected to ~ port unit of each pair of turbo-jet powerplants. One hundred ninety-three B-52G's rolled off the ~chita production line with the first aircraft coming ~ the line on October 17, 1958. The G variant in~rporated extensive changes with a redesigned ~ng containing internal fuel tanks. The fuel capacity ~s increased to a whopping 46,000 gallons. A ~nificant tactical change had the gunner position~ forward in the pressurized forward portion of the ~rcraft. The B-52G also demonstrated 25% greater ~nge, increased climb performance and greater ~er-target altitude. But the most noticeable out~rd change was the shortening of the vertical fin, a ~ange which would also be carried through to the ~al H version.

To demonstrate its improved capability, an Air ~rce manned B-52G landed at Edwards Air Force ~se, California, to complete a 28 hour, non-stop ~ght of almost 13,000 miles. The B-52G actually ~tered SAC service in February 1959. A B-52G ~ed with turbo-fan engines and serving as a flying ~t bed for the H Model, flew for the first time in ~ly 1960.

The B-52H would be the last of the Stratofort ~eed with Wichita production (September 1960 to ~ctober 1962) turning out 102 of the Model. The B-~H was a radical improvement over its earlier

brothers with the equipping of P&W TF-33 turbo-fans. The advanced powerplants gave the B-52H a 10-15% increase in range. The new power boost made the H Model seem like a new airplane. An operational B-52H demonstrated the improved capability with a 12,500 mile non-stop trip from Okinawa to Madrid, Spain in less than 22 hours to set or break 11 distance course and speed records without refueling. Another advancement also oc-curred with the substitution of the 6,000 round per minute six-barrel Gatling Gun replacing the original four-gun tail-turret armament.

Although the B-52G and B-52H are very similar in appearance, they differ greatly internally. In addi-tion to the improved powerplants, the H Model con-tains advanced low altitude capabilities and ad-ditional crew comfort provisions for long duration flights.

Although the B-52H was the last model to be produced, diring the mid-1970's another (the B-52I) was mentioned as a possible future B-52 variant. The B-52I was, however, not to be a new airframe production program but rather an extensive modification of the B-52G/H fleet. The modification would incorporate new more powerful engines and new electronics technology. Boeing estimates ranged from 7 to 12 million dollars per airplane for the "upgrading." At the time of this writing (early 1975), there had been no firm decision made as to whether the modification would be made.

montage of B-52 models and paint jobs can be seen on the Kelly Air Force Base flight line. Three *different* paint schemes are visible—the plain bare metal and two camouflage schemes. (USAF Photo)

## MODIFICATIONS

In an operational career of some two decades in 1975, the B-52 has maintained its role as SAC's front-line strategic bomber. Perhaps the most important reasons the Stratofortress can claim such longevity are the Air Force's and Boeing's extensive modification programs. Historically, maintenance and modification of B-52's has rested with the Oklahoma City Air Logistics Center at Tinker Air Force Base and the San Antonio Air Logistics Center at Kelly AFB.

One of the largest B-52 modifications, the "Mod 1000" low level capability, was the largest single modification ever initiated on any weapon system by the U.S. Air Force in the 1960's. It equipped various models of the B-52 to perform high speed, low level penetration flights with an air-to-surface missile profile while still maintaining its high altitude capability.

Other modifications made during the 1960's included addition of various missile carrying capabilities and electronic counter measure systems to counter increased sophistication of enemy air-defense capabilities. All these modification requirements were met as a matter of course. Since the B-52 maintenance program began at San Antonio, more than 1,500 B-52's have been overhauled there (as of 1974).

Providing the Stratofortress with adequate structural integrity became a problem of great magnitude in the 1960's as the bomber approached the end of its structural life span. Engineering changes to beef-up structural weaknesses were developed to guard against further deterioration and fatigue. As a result, the life of the B-52 was extended to meet continued operational commitments.

The 1960's also brought forth other changes which increased the effectiveness of the B-52. With America's involvement in the Vietnam conflict, the

Air Force required the heavy bomber in a conv[entional] tional role. Although the B-52's were able to ca[rry] both conventional and nuclear bombs, the Strato[for-] tresses were limited in the quantity of conventio[nal] bombs they could carry.

In 1963, plans were developed to expand the c[on-] ventional capabilities of the heavy bomber. F[our] years later, at the peak of the Vietnam conflict, [B-] 52's were capable of dropping a much grea[ter] payload than their originally designed capaci[ty.] Looking at this achievement from another persp[ec-] tive, modified B-52D's each had the equivalent c[on-] ventional bombing power of four unmodified a[ir-] craft. Each modified bomber could drop 30 tons [of] iron bombs.

Another large modification effort was the B-[52] quick start package. This modification installed ca[r-] tridge/pneumatic starters on all eight engines on [B-] 52G/H aircraft which allowed the simultaneous sta[r-] ting of all engines. The program, which began [in] 1974 was scheduled for completion in 1976. Tw[o] hundred and seventy-three aircraft were to [be] modified.

USAF's big AFLC maintenance hangar at San A[n-] tonio, built in 1955, was the scene of many B-[52] modification programs. The building, covering o[ne] million square feet of floor space, can accommoda[te] some 16 B-52's at one time. Enhancement of B-[52] structural integrity and increased B-52 payloa[d] were results of the work.

As the future of the Stratofortress is examined, t[he] continued use of the B-52 is well into the 198[0's] seems assured. The aircraft even though its desi[gn] roots go back to the 1940's has benefited from t[he] new aircraft technology of the 1960's and 1970['s.] The B-52's today in the SAC fleet are far bett[er] weapon systems than they were the day they we[re] built!

# Chapter III
# Many Jobs—Master of All

Versatility and flexibility are but two of the superlatives that can be applied to the B-52. Its longevity has seen it serve in many capacities beyond that for which it was initially conceived. Designed to perform a high altitude nuclear deterrance function, the Stratofort has performed a multitude of undesigned-for functions including carrying ballistic and cruise stand-off missiles, air-breathing decoy missiles and conventional iron bombs. And in addition to the tactical implications of the B-52, a small number of B-52's have performed important functions in aeronautical and space research programs.

The B-52 was designed from the off-set as a delivery system of nuclear bombs. It has retained this capability. But a whole host of new weapon innovations have been added. And there could be additional new weapons before the last Stratofort is retired.

This B-52 stand-off role is best typified by the AGM-28B jet powered Hound Dog missiles the Stratofort has carried in pairs since 1960. The Hound Dogs are carried on wing-mounted pylons between the fuselage and inboard engines. The missiles extend the operations reach of the B-52 by more than 500 miles and permit one bomber to knock out several targets hundreds of miles apart. The Hound Dog's inertial navigation system is pre-set for a mission but can be re-targeted prior to its release from the aircraft. The 42 foot long missile can fly at 50,000 foot altitudes at a speed of 1,200 MPH. A unique B-52/Hound Dog interplay occurs as the Hound Dog's 7,500 pound thrust engines can be used to augment the B-52 thrust in flight. The Hound Dogs' tanks can then be refilled in flight from the B-52 tanks.

*Early artist's concept showing an early Hound Dog being launched by a B-52 of unknown model.*
*(Boeing Photo)*

*One of this B-52G's Hound Dog Missiles falls free in a flight test. (USAF Photo)*

*Pylon mount of the two Hound-Dog missiles is very clear in this picture. The missiles' engines can be used to augment the bomber's thrust when the extra thrust is needed      (Boeing Photo)*

*An overall view of a B-52H carrying four dummy Skybolt missiles. The program was quite advanced for the time period and would have made the B-52H a fantastic stand-off weapon had the program been allowed to continue to completion.*
*(Boeing Photo)*

*Almost a half million pounds of B-52H and its external load of SRAM missiles is maneuvered into position.*                                                        *(USAF Photo)*

In February 1960, the Air Force approved
evelopment of a long range ballistic missile that
ould be launched against ground targets from
igh-flying jet bombers . . . a weapon more
ophisticated with more accuracy and range (1,150
iles) than any previous air-to-surface missile. The
issile was called the Skybolt (GAM-87A) and the
arrying bombers were to be the B-52H and RAF
ulcan jet bombers. Each Stratofort was to carry
our Skybolts, two under each wing on inverted T
ylons. But the program was soon to be cancelled
nd the B-52H's were adapted to carry the Hound
og.

Some 281 B-52G and B-52H Models were
odified to carry the next of the montage of
eapon systems. The Short Range Attack Missile
AGM-69A SRAM) provided a new dimension to the
-52's offensive strike capability. The SRAM is a 14
oot long missile weighing only 2,230 pounds. Iner-
ally guided, the missile is powered by a two-pulse,
olid-propellant rocket motor and carries a nuclear
arhead. It can be re-targeted aboard the aircraft
rior to launch. Both the B-52, FB-111 and upcoming
-1 bomber can carry the SRAM. The B-52 can carry
o to 20 SRAM's on wing pylons and a rotary
auncher singly or in salvo demonstrating a variety
f trajectories from different directions. Sixteen B-52
nd two FB-111 units are programmed to be
quipped with the SRAM.

As the B-52's aged through the 1960's and into
the 1970's, significant electronic improvements were
incorporated in the Stratoforts. One of the most
significant countermeasures carried for some time
was the ADM-20 Quail decoy missile. Some 245 of
the small diversionary missiles were ordered. The jet
powered decoys were to be dropped in an
operational environment from the Stratofort's bomb
bays. The Quail's electronics would then simulate a
B-52 to enemy radar scopes. Additional
decoy/diversion gear was carried by some B-52's in
the form of chaff dispensing pods. These pods are
located on a wing pylon between the engine pods. In
the pods, 2.75 inch rockets actually push chaff out-
ward in front of the aircraft for radar deception.

SCAD was the acronym for Subsonic Cruise Arm-
ed Decoy which was to be the replacement for the
Quail but with one added dimension. The SCAD was
to, in addition to its decoy mission, carry a warhead.
The SCAD was to have been launched from the
SRAM launcher.

The program was initiated in June 1972, and was
cancelled in early 1974. During 1974, an air-
launched cruise missile with a diversional mission
was being considered to replace the cancelled
SCAD.

During 1973, with the installation of the Electro-
optical Viewing System (EVS), the B-52G/H's offensive capabilities were greatly increased in darkness.

*The Rotary Rapid-Launch equipment in the B-52's weapons bay gives the plane unprecedented ability to penetrate heavily defended targets using the SRAM missile. SRAM can attack from low or high altitude, behind or to the side of the carrying aircraft and can be launched at supersonic speeds.* *(Boeing Photo)*

46

Close-up of inboard pylon installation carrying SRAM's

(USAF Photo)

External configuration of the Air Force's new AGM-69A SRAM is shown to good advantage on this

*This B-52H, which was involved in the SRAM test program, sports the standard camouflage paint job. This includes the two-shade green combination on the upper portion of the aircraft and the white underside.* *(Boeing Photo)*

*About the mid-1960's, a new paint job started appearing. This Wichita-built B-52D shows its shiny black underside and black vertical fin. Engine bottoms and fuel tank bottoms also got the sinister black look.* *(Boeing Photo)*

*The B-52D was the most numerous of the Stratoforts to be produced. This particular aircraft SN 0-60684, is painted in the two-tone green and black paint job. The D Model was used extensively in Vietnam.* *(USAF Photo)*

*Shown is a test flight of a B-52D dropping conventional iron bombs in a Boeing test. As many as 84 500 pounders mounted in three racks can be quickly installed in the bomb bay. An additional 24 more 750 pounders can be carried externally on racks attached to pylons which are located under the wings.* *(Boeing Photo)*

*A beautiful picture of a B-52G sporting two Hound Dog missiles.* (Boeing Photo)

*Standing as a monument at Anderson Air Force Base in Guam, this B-52 Stratofort serves as a reminder of the contribution the B-52 made in the Vietnam War. This particular Stratofort participated in four missions over North Vietnam in Project Linebacker II.* (USAF Photo)
*The B-52D was the most numerous of the Stratoforts to be produced. This particular aircraft SN 0-60684, is painted in the two-tone green and black paint job. The D Model was used extensively in Vietnam.* (USAF Photo)

*Six SRAM's can be seen being carried on the inboard pylon installation on a B-52H bomber. The Stratofortress can also carry the missile internally. (USAF Photo)*

58

The EVS kits were designed to increase the effectiveness of the G and H models of the Stratofortress by providing the crew with an improved flight hazard avoidance capability which enables the airplanes to fly low level in a "closed curtain" environment. It also allows the crew to assess strike target damage and avoid low level terrain features. The Electro-optical Viewing System consists of two steerable sensors: one a low-light-level TV camera, and the other an infrared unit. They are mounted in turrets under the nose of the B-52. Looking forward and downward, they transmit a picture of the terrain in TV display form to the cockpit and navigator stations. Boeing-Wichita conducted feasibility studies and tests of the viewing system during the 1966-68 period and completed a successful prototype flight test program in 1969-70. Production kit deliveries began in October 1972, and the Strategic Air Command received its first EVS-equipped aircraft in February 1973. Delivery of the last kit will take place in 1976.

But with increasing American involvement in Vietnam during the 1960's, the massive capability of the B-52 as an iron bomb hauler was explored. On June 18, 1965, modified B-52's started carrying out high altitude missions against targets in South Vietnam. Modifications on the Stratoforts by Boeing had increased conventional bombing capabilities by as much as 57% on some of the models.

Modification of the bomb bay permitted loadings of up to 84 bombs in the 500-pound class, or 42 750-pounders. An additional 24 750-pounders could be carried on external racks under the wings. B-52's so equipped were able to carry a total bombload of about 60,000 pounds—an increase of 31,750 pounds over the 28,250 pound normal payload. Another benefit derived from the modification was the ability to convert the aircraft's bomb-carrying equipment from nuclear to non-nuclear configurations and back.

Although it couldn't be classed as a modification of the significance of the aforementioned examples, the B-52 models have seen several different paint schemes. The initial Stratoforts rolled out in bare metal until the mid-1950's when a special thermal-reflective paint was applied to the exposed under side of the aircraft. Then, starting in 1965, SAC Stratoforts started going into the paint shops to receive a two-shade green and tan upper, and white underside, camouflage. However, it wasn't long before an additional variation appeared with a shiney black finish being applied to the normally white underbelly portion and vertical fin. The black finish and absence of markings gave the once nuclear bomber a bit of a "back-woods" look.

But not all of the B-52's modifications have been for tactical or strategic reasons. The aircraft has served as a test bed aircraft for many programs.

The ADM-20 Quail diversionary missile was carried for a number of years by the B-52 fleet. With its electronic equipment, it was able to simulate a B-52 on a radar scope.(McDonnellDouglas Photo)

An artist's concept of the Cancelled SCAD missile being launched from a B-52. Not only did the SCAD

The United States Air Force currently is developing the Air Launched Cruise Missile (ALCM) as an adjunct to the Nation's strategic bomber force. The air-to-ground ALCM will be interchangeable with the Short Range Attack Missile (SRAM) and carried internally by the B-52 and B-1.

Primary differences between the ALCM and SRAM are speed, range and terminal accuracy. The ALCM will be approximately the same size as the SRAM, with first flight planned for mid-1976.

The ALCM will extend bomber target coverage, enhance bomber penetration and serve as a back-up against the possibility of reduced or lost tanker support. The missile will carry a nuclear warhead and be equipped with an internal navigation and guidance system.

The new ALCM is based on the design of the terminated Subsonic Cruise Armed Decoy (SCAD) and will benefit from the development, testing and design work already completed on that program. Because so much of the development work already has been accomplished, the Air Force is able to move relatively quickly with development of ALCM.                    (USAF Photo)

A technician works on the tail armament which is carried by all B-52's except the final H Model. The tail cannons are the only guns which are carried on the B-52's. *(USAF Photo)*

*A fire control system capable of firing 20mm cannon shells at the rate of 4,000 rounds per minute through a Gatling gun was installed in the B-52H for tail armament. Its high firing rate is achieved by the use of six revolving barrels, each with its own bolt.*

*(Boeing Photo)*

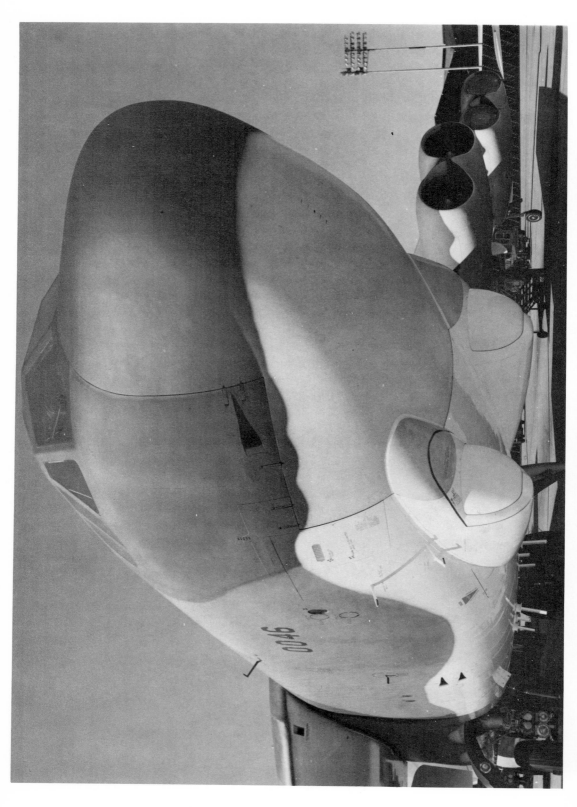

*The installation of the EVS System is shown in its location under the forward portion of the fuselage.*

Probably the most famous payload that the B-52 has been a "Mother Ship" for is the X-15 rocket powered research vehicle. The "Manned Rocket" set many altitude records before the space era began. (NASA Photo)

*Falling free, the X-15 rocket ship's rocket engine is being brought to life which would push it to the*

Another of the many and varied B-52 research payloads was the NASA HL-10 lifting body. The installation of this craft under the B-52 was very similar to the X-15 installation.     (NASA Photo)

The X-24 lifting body is air launched from a B-52 mother ship flying at 45,000 feet. The wingless craft is being used in the development of a space shuttle craft.     (NASA Photo)

The X-24 is a joint NASA/USAF project. This picture shows the details of the installation of the vehi-

*A three-eighths scale model of the F-15 fighter was flight tested under the wing of the B-52 mother ship. The model was air-launched from the B-52 at 45,000 feet and commands were transmitted to the unmanned vehicle from the ground.*
*(NASA Photo)*

*A B-52E which was equipped to perform testing of the new engine for the Boeing 747. Another B-52 was similarly equipped to test the new engine for the C-5A.*

*(Pratt and Whitney Photo)*

Probably the best known B-52 applications are as "mother ship" carriers for a number of the famous X family of high performance craft. The B-52 continues to be used in this research role. The manned rocket powered, manned X-15 was probably the best known of the B-52 "riders." More recently, the so-called NB-52 has been used to carry the X-24 family of hypersonic research vehicles. This job could carry well into the late 1970's.

During 1973, an NB-52E participated in a test program to produce super-stable aircraft of the future. The Stratofort was equipped with a series of forward canards. The CCV (Control Configured Vehicle) program demonstrated that the speed of future aircraft need not be limited to avoid flutter or structural bending. The CCV modifications on the NB-52E enabled it to surpass its design flutter speed a number of times.

Two other B-52's served as test beds for large new jet engines. The TF-39 (engine for the Lockheed C-5A) and the JT9D (engine for the Boeing 747) were both flight tested on modified Stratofortresses. The installations were basically identical with the huge new engines mounted on the right inboard engine pylons.

Then there are B-52's turning up in the strangest places. A salvaged late model B-52 fuselage was used at the Rome Air Development Center for the purpose of making antenna pattern measurements. Then in 1974, a surplus B-52D served as a test bed for a Boeing structural test. The test airplane, with its nose and tail removed, was inverted and placed in a support structure. Then the test instrumentation was added, the wing was loaded with lead shot and sandbags until the wing failed. The wing loading data provided data on the strength of fleet B-52's.

*The GE powerplant for the Lockheed C-5A was tested on a B-52 inboard pylon.    (GE Photo)*

An excess B-52D aircraft was used in a special wing loading test at the Boeing Wichita plant. The test

*B-52's just seem to keep appearing in the strangest places. At the Air Force's Rome Air Development Center a B-52G is being used in radar measurement testing.* (USAF Photo)

*During 1973, a B-52 was modified in order to carry out a series of flight control tests. The test air craft, which was called the NB-52E, was equipped with a long nose-mounted test probe and three small canards located on the forward portion of the fuselage.* (USAF Photo)

73

# Chapter IV

# SAC's Big Stick—the B-52

In order to perpetrate the strategic bombing superiority that had helped bring the victory during World War II, the Strategic Air Command was formed on March 21, 1946.

General George C. Kenney was appointed commander and given the mandate of building an organization capable of conducting long-range offensive operations in any part of the world. He began with a total of 37,000 military men and 950 aircraft—about 300 of which were vintage B-17's, B-25's and B-29's. Four months after he started, the atomic bomb test at Bikini displayed the command's nuclear capability and ushered in an era of rapid expansion and build-up.

In 1948, two new aircraft were delivered—the B-36 and B-50—and General Curtis E. LeMay took command. The headquarters moved from Andrews AFB, Maryland, to Offutt AFB, Nebraska, and in-flight refueling was introduced, giving SAC's bombers true "intercontinental" range.

During the Korean War, SAC B-29's made history in their first real test of combat readiness, dropping 167,000 tons of conventional bombs and destroying every strategic industrial target in North Korea in three months. In August 1953, the explosion of the first Soviet hydrogen bomb emphasized the red nuclear threat and all phases of SAC training were pushed ahead at full speed.

New aircraft were swiftly introduced to replace older obsolete systems. By the mid-fifties, the first all-jet B-47 bomber had replaced the B-29's and B-50's and the KC-97 was the main refueling tanker. In 1955, the B-52 made its appearance on the SAC scene. By the end of the 1950's, a portion of the B-52

*The exciting SAC alerts of an earlier time. Note the lack of camouflage paint on the two B-52's that are visible.*
*(USAF Photo)*

A B-52 of undetermined model takes off for a long airborne alert mission. During the later years with

A B-52H takes on fuel from a KC-135. There have been literally tens of thousands of these B-52 refueling operations since the B-52 became operational. (USAF Photo)

*The FB-111 is a companion aircraft to the B-52 fleet. The picture shows the aircraft mounting four*

750 pounders are loaded on outside pylon. These are in addition to additional bombs which are carried internally.
(USAF Photo)

*A sight which was seen only during the early days of B-52 operations—that being a B-52 being refueled by a KC-97. Note the upward attitude of the B-52 in order to match speed with the tanker.* *(USAF Photo)*

*An early model B-52 appears to be in a climbing attitude as it takes on fuel from a KC-135.* *(USAF Photo)*

Many B-52's came back to the states during their Southeast Asian tours for modification and rework. This veteran, as can be attested from its many mission markings, receives attention at Kelly

Many engines were removed from B-52's in storage at Davis-Monthan Air Force Base and sent to Vietnam where they were used in B-52's making bombing missions. This picture shows an engine removal operation under way on a Stratofort at the Arizona facility.　　　　(USAF Photo)

The flying boom of a KC-135 tanker aircraft fills up a B-52 on its way to drop its load in Vietnam. Note the external pylons loaded with conventional ordnance.　　　　(USAF Photo)

bomber force was on 15-minute ground alert, and airborne alert and dispersal concepts were being tested to combat decreasing warning times.

It was the standard practice for some time that a certain percentage of the B-52 force would always be airborne. This practice proved impractical for a number of reasons, and a ground alert system with super-quick response times was developed. The ground alert technique continues to be employed in the mid-1970's.

The B-52's first chance to respond during a war-threatening situation came in 1962 during the Cuban missile crisis. During this tense time, SAC began dispersing aircraft, moving a number of its Florida-based B-52 bombers and KC-135 tankers to other U.S. bases to make room for the tactical aircraft build-up there.

On October 25, 1962, SAC's help was required in locating Soviet surface shipping, and SAC B-47 reconnaissance aircraft and KC-97 tankers began combing an 825,000 square mile rectangle north of Cuba between Bermuda and the Azores. Hundreds of visual and radar sightings were made from high altitudes to as low as 300 feet on these missions. Initial contact with the Soviet ships, however, had been made within hours by B-52 aircraft flying airborne alert missions.

The most significant of all the manned weapon system activities, however, was this: the Strategic Air Command launched the first airborne alert in the history of airpower, as a number of B-52's took to the air on 24-hour missions designed to keep them within reach of potential targets at all times.

This airborne alert guaranteed the survival of large part of SAC's strike aircraft from any attack including one without warning. From its beginning October 22 to its end November 21, when routine airborne alert training was resumed, SAC bombers and tankers flew more than 2,000 sorties calling for nearly 50,000 hours of continuous flight. Under constant positive control, airborne alert aircraft flew more than 20 million miles and transferred some 7 million gallons of fuel during more than 4,000 aerial refuelings.

Almost three years later, the Stratofort was called on again and this time it was for real. From June 18 1965 to January 27, 1973, B-52's flew conventional bombing missions almost daily against Communist forces in Vietnam. Crews on temporary duty from their home bases in the United States and operating from U-Tapao, Thailand, and Andersen AFB, Guam flew B-52's each carrying up to 60,000 pounds of bombs to perform strategic bombing, close air support, and interdiction missions. B-52 strikes continued against military targets in Laos until April 17 1973, and in support of friendly forces in Cambodia until August 15, 1973.

During its wide-ranging operations in South Vietnam, the B-52's were used to deliver huge tonnage of bombs in precision high altitude strikes against

The "Lady Luck", which participated in 102 combat missions. The aircraft was stationed on Guam attached to the 454th Bomb Wing.
(AF Museum Photo)

84

A B-52 lands at Kadena Air Base, Okinawa, on February 5, 1968, after a mission over Southeast Asia.

(USAF Photo)

idden enemy concentrations. Usually flying in three plane cells, the B-52's helped clear paths for tactical round operations against targets that were usually well hidden. The target types included supply zones, rea headquarters and troop concentrations.

With the late 1960's, build-up of U.S. forces in outheast Asia, the Stratoforts increased their raids n support of ground operations. Raids concentrated n such areas as the demilitarized zone where the nemy was attempting to move supplies to the south.

B-52's played an important part in the now-amous Khe Sanh operation. Early in 1968, 6,000 Marines and South Vietnamese Rangers were sur-ounded at this austere outpost by 20,000 North ietnamese troops. While tactical fighters harassed ne enemy, the B-52's dropped up to 1,400 tons of rdnance daily with devastating results. The effec-veness of the B-52 response was intensified by the rrival of a three-plane cell every 90 minutes round ne clock. During the Khe Sanh operations, the tratoforts rose for some 2,600 sorties delivering ver 75,000 tons of ordnance. The nuclear bomber ad demonstrated with conventional ordnance the ffectiveness of WWII saturation bombing.

But the biggest operation for the B-52's would ome in December 1972. The mission would be up orth and the challenge would be the toughest the ld bird would probably ever face. The targets ould be installations and transshipment points near anoi and Haiphong in North Vietnam. It was

hoped that the "Linebacker II" operation would br-ing an end to American involvement in Vietnam. A little-known fact is that this was not the first time the B-52's had ventured north. During the previous April 17, B-52's attacked targets near Haiphong with all aircraft returning safely.

B-52's had previously been under SAM attack in southern operations but they had been few and scattered. Linebacker II would provide a massive SAM challenge, along with the menace of fighters, for the first time to the B-52. As it worked out, there were no Stratofort losses to MiG's although some 32 came up to contest the B-52's.

The raids were carried out during eleven fateful days—18 through the 29th of December. The Stratoforts (namely B-52D's and B-52G's) went in at night to prevent visual tracking. But the B-52's prov-ed to be just as effective at night. Flying Linebacker II during daylight hours wouldn't have afforded any advantage since the miserable weather would have afforded only 12 hours when visual bombing could have been accomplished.

Linebacker II was a team effort; a highly coor-dinated and precision-run operation. Navy tactical aircraft and Marine fighters provided a protective combat screen and attacked targets near the coast. Air Force fighters provided protective escort for the B-52, combat air patrol, and defensive suppression for the Hanoi-Haiphong complex. The B-52's also used chaff ECM to confuse the enemy defenses.

CONVENTIONAL BOMBING—This camouflaged B-52D Stratofortress releases its 60,000 pound bomb load of "iron bombs" on enemy targets in Vietnam. Each B-52 can carry up to eighty-four 500-pound bombs or forty-two 750-pound bombs internally and twenty-four 750-pound bombs exter-

Loading operations as second "Stratofortress" waits its turn.     (USAF Photo)

(USAF Photo)

Loading outside bomb pylons.

*Two Southeast Asian Boeing partners meet on the flight line. The helicopter is the Boeing Vertol CH-46A Sea Knight which saw action in Vietnam. The B-52 is an F model which shines with a new paint job.*
*(Boeing Photo)*

Railroad targets were hit first with some 383 rail cars, 14 locomotives, 191 warehouses and two bridges destroyed. In addition, of the nine major storage areas in the general bombing area, 25 major, 26 small and 29 other buildings were destroyed. The bombing was accurate and decisive. During the operation, over 20,000 tons were dropped—mostly by the B-52's. But the cost was not cheap. Fifteen of the giant Stratoforts were lost, 10 of which went down in North Vietnamese territory. Nine other forts were damaged (two heavily) but all of these made it back safely. The cost had been high, but not as high as had been estimated. Losses had been estimated at three percent. As it worked out, the loss amounted to only two percent (15 aircraft, on about 700 sorties). But the cost was still high! Very high! But the B-52's got the job done.

# e Stratofort—
# m the Cockpit

very plane that was ever built got a nickname or
. For the B-52, it is the unlikely title of BUFF. The
nym surprisingly stands for "Big Ugly Fat
w." Where the name came from isn't clear but it
ably originated sometime during the mid-
0's in South East Asia.

ven in the 1970's, the "big" aspect of the B-52 is
true. And even in the era of the C-5A and 747
oo-jets, the B-52 is still an impressive aircraft.
h her long sweeping swept wings and arching
she belies her 1940's heritage. But even though
pilots saw fit to slip in "Ugly" in her "BUFF"
nym, the old bird has a majestic and domineer-
beauty about her. She's like the lines of a classic
—they never seem to get out of date.

Walking about the aircraft, one can't help but be
impressed with the protrusions and hang-ons which
the bird seems to bristle with. The 52's eight engines,
which are mounted in pairs, are carried in sharply
forward-raked pods under the thin high speed wing.
The stepped-diameter turbofans of the final H Model
are quite distinguishable from the trim lines of the
earlier engines.

The fuselage-mounted gear arrangement appears
insignificant when compared to the massive weight it
is supporting. The small outriggers on the wingtips
barely plant themselves when the wings of a G or H
Model are bulging with fuel. When the wings are
dry, the outriggers hang helplessly grasping for the
ground they can't reach. The riggers do, however,

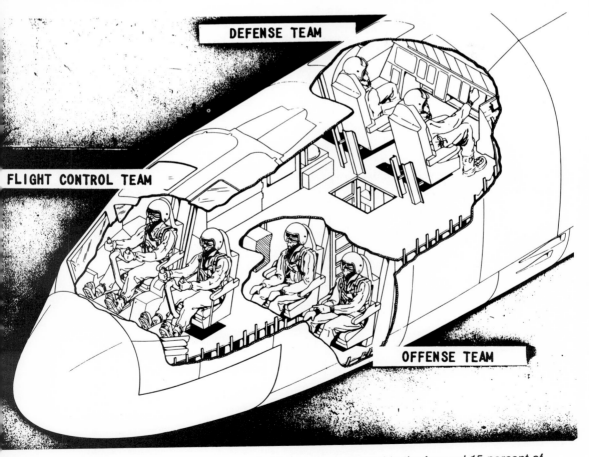

52G and B-52H crew positions. The six-man B-52 crew is positioned in the forward 15 percent of
e aircraft.

(USAF Photo)

*The slight upsweep of one of the engine pods is quite obvious in this photo.* (Dale Witt Photo)

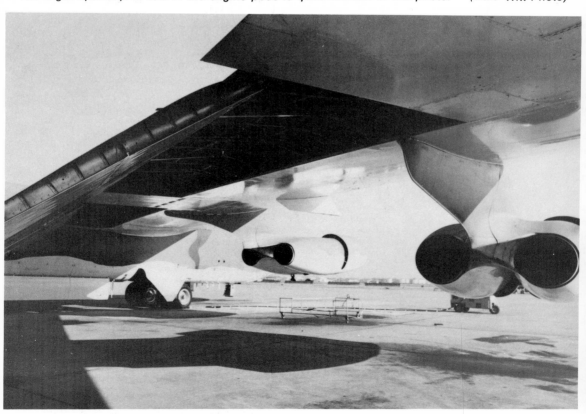

*A rear view of the B-52H's giant turbo-fan powerplants.* (Dale Witt Photo)

*With her fuel tanks loaded (note outriggers on ground) and drag chute deployed, this B-52G rolls in for a landing.* *(Boeing Photo)*

end to keep the plane from tipping when the plane is moving. BUFF pilots like to refer to them as "training wheels."

The immense size of the giant Fowler Flaps is staggering when they hang in their fully extended position. The flaps are fully extended for both take-off and landing. The function they perform is closely tied with the unique landing gear arrangement. Since the gears are in tandem, the B-52 must land aft gear first. If the forward gear hits first, the Stratofort has a tendency to skip back into the air. The giant flaps are needed to provide necessary lift.

The B-52 is a strange combination of the very strong and very weak. The aircraft was built to carry massive bomb loads over intercontinental distances. She is far from being a high-G aircraft being only stressed for about two G's. A B-52 pilot aptly described the B-52 fuselage as a pencil. "It can be pushed and pulled as long as the forces are applied along the fuselage centerline. But put a side pressure on it and it can be easily broken." The maximum skin thickness of the B-52 is 0.40 inches.

A testament, however, to the B-52's strength and stamina occurred during a mid-1960's test flight of a B-52G. A violent gust tore away the airplane's rudder and most of the vertical fin. But even so, the craft was able to make a safe landing 700 miles later.

Crawling into the innards of this behemoth, one quickly realizes how little actual room there is for the crew. The complete crew of six is stationed in the forward 15 percent of the aircraft. The missions are long and tiring. And the "living area" is extremely small for the crew of six compared to the overall size of the airplane. Ejection from the aircraft is upward for the four crew members on the upper deck, while the other two are shot out the bottom of the plane. The remainder of the bird, the majority of which is the weapons-carrying section, is not pressurized.

The cockpit is a cozy arrangement with a myriad of panels and instruments surrounding the pilot and co-pilot. Located between the seats are the eight throttles for the eight engines. The pre-flight checklist for flight is long, covering many pages.

Take-off in the B-52 is one of the strangest characteristics of this giant bird. The B-52 does not rotate as it leaves the ground. It looks more like it's going up on an elevator. And as the eight wheels of the main gear leave the ground, the aircraft fuselage remains practically level. One wonders where the lift comes from. But looking at the way the wing is joined to the fuselage and the giant flaps explains this apparently strange flight phenomenon. The design of the Fowler Flaps give the aircraft high lift during take-offs and landings with zero fuselage angle. So, even though the fuselage can even have a nose down attitude, bringing the wings to the level position, the plane can maintain level flight. The Stratofort is indeed a unique flying machine.

*The giant Fowler Flap (inboard) is shown in the fully extended position. Rear wheels of main gear can also be seen.*
                                                                                    *(Dale Witt Photo)*

*Flight line shot of the 17th Bomb Wing, 2nd Air Force at Wright Patterson Air Force Base. All the equipment that can be seen are B-52H's with the exception of one B-52F.*
                                                                                    *(Photo by Walter Halfacre)*

The low sweeping lines of the B-52H still look good today. (Author Photo)

The B52H's main gear arrangement can be seen in this picture. It is imperative that both sets of wheels hit together on landing.                                                    (Dale Witt Photo)

*Close-up view of R*
*Operator's console.*
*(Dale Witt Ph*

*View of the console*
*the Radar Operator o*
*left and the Navigato*
*the right.*
*(Dale Witt P*

*Sitting in the B*
*cockpit, Major*
*Chamblee explains t*
*tricacies of flying*
*Stratofort to the auth*
*(Dale Witt P*

Major Chamblee shows the author the workings of the B-52H weapons compartment. Pair are standing under the open bomb bay. (Dale Witt Photo)

The deadly tail stinger of the B-52H. The photo also emphasizes the height of the Stratofort's vertical fin. (Dale Witt Photo)

Major Buzz Chamblee, 17th Bomb Wing, illustrates the size of the front portion of the B-52H's main gear. (Dale Witt Photo)

*Good place to take a nap. SAC ground maintenance man illustrates the size of the turbofan in-takes.*
*(Dale Witt Photo)*

Lifting off the runway, the Stratofort seems to first test the air for lift, starting at the wingtips. Then the vast expanse of wing, some 4,000 square feet, starts to take the hint and arches toward the fuel and bomb-laden fuselage. Slowly the fuselage fights the bonds of earth bringing the gear struts up to maximum deflection till the rubber leaves the concrete.

The procedures for getting B-52's airborne through the G Models, and then the B-52H, are entirely different. To get the non-turbofan equipped (A-G) Stratoforts off the ground, hundreds of gallons of water are injected through the eight engines for added thrust. It would be almost impossible to get a fully-loaded B-52 off the ground without this additional augmentation.

But with the B-52H, it's an entirely different situation. With each of its turbofans kicking out some 17,-000 pounds of thrust, the H Model has power to burn. In fact, even when fully loaded, the B-52H

doesn't even need to use maximum power settings for a heavy-weight take-off. The B-52H take-off is characterized by relatively constant acceleration throughout the range of take-off weights which is accomplished by adjusting the throttle settings. For a light-weight take-off, the take-off speed is about 127 knots, while a heavy-weight load needs about 160 knots to clear the runway.

The B-52H can, with its great power reserve, easily handle the situation of losing an engine during take-off. The pilot maneuvers the rudder and juggles the throttles to take care of the thrust imbalance. Loss of an outboard engine is, of course, a more critical situation.

B-52 pilots who flew the early model B-52's tell of the muscular operations required with the operation of the manual flight control system. But the B-52G/H Models show improvement in this area being extremely light on the stick. There are no trim tabs on the H Model.

The contrails from eight turbofan engines flair out from the rear of a B-52H Stratofort. Note the Hound Dog missiles which are clearly visible. (Boeing Photo)

A 1969 occurrence when a B-52 crew landed their "six-engine" Stratofort at Wurtsmith AFB, Michigan, after engine 5 and 6 burned and dropped off, and 7 and 8 ran out of fuel. (USAF Photo)

One of the most famous B-52 pictures ever taken. This B-52H, on a test flight, encountered severe turbulence and lost its rudder and most of the vertical fin. It still was able to make a safe landing. (USAF Photo)

In flight, the B-52 is an extremely stable aircraft. The main reason for this stability is the tremendous weight and inertia of the plane. Once 240 tons of Stratofort is pointed in one direction, it doesn"t want to change. Pilots tell that the big bird takes turbulence and weather very smoothly. The pilots tell of the B-52's great inertia coming into play during refueling operations. The tremendous inertia of the B-52's heavier weight ranges causes it to be less responsive to pilot inputs throughout the complete refueling sequence. The B-52G/H's can be refueled from 200,000—488,000 pounds—a weight range in excess of 100 tons.

The B-52 cannot maneuver with most other aircraft. This lack of maneuverability once again can be related to its great weight and range. The B-52H, for example, can fly some twenty hours on its internal fuel supply alone.

Getting the Stratofortress stopped after touchdown is another problem which faced the Boeing engineers. The B-52 carries a formidable braking system. Translated into layman realities, the brakes absorb enough energy to stop, simultaneously, 470 automobiles traveling at 50 MPH. Under full braking conditions, the energy absorbed would halt over 1,-000 cars. The B-52, drawing from a similar application on the earlier B-47, also uses a braking parachute deployed from the rear of the aircraft.

The B-52 is a very forgiving aircraft—certainly much more than say the B-47 or the B-58 bomber aircraft. The big wings, adequate power and a super-strong landing gear help cover mistakes. Another aspect of B-52 safety is that each different B-52 seems to act almost identically with each of its Stratofortress brothers. This is an extremely important detail since, unlike the World War II days, each crew draws whatever aircraft is ready and not the same one every time.

But it should probably be noted in conclusion that the B-52 is not a pilot's airplane. It was an airplane built to be "directed" by the navigator and radar operator to a point where the ordnance could be put on the target. It was built initially as a high altitude nuclear bomber, then modified as a high-altitude mount for stand-off weapons, and finally as a carrier of conventional ordnance.

The Stratofort has only had an opportunity to perform in the last role, a role that was conjured up in a short time. But even so, it did its job well. Great job—BUFF!

*A B-52G sporting its 400 pounds of camouflage paint. Note the droop of the wing pressing the outrigger to the concrete indicating that the fuel cells in the wings are filled.* (USAF Photo)

101

*Oklahoma City, the site of so much of the B-52 modification work down through the years, saw fit to honor the Stratofort. This B-52 rests on a series of pylons ahead of a B-47. She has earned a place*

*Roll-out of the Rockwell International B-1 swept-wing bomber. SAC has high hopes for this advanced aircraft to be the ultimate replacement of the B-52. Pictured is the 1974 roll-out.* (USAF Photo)

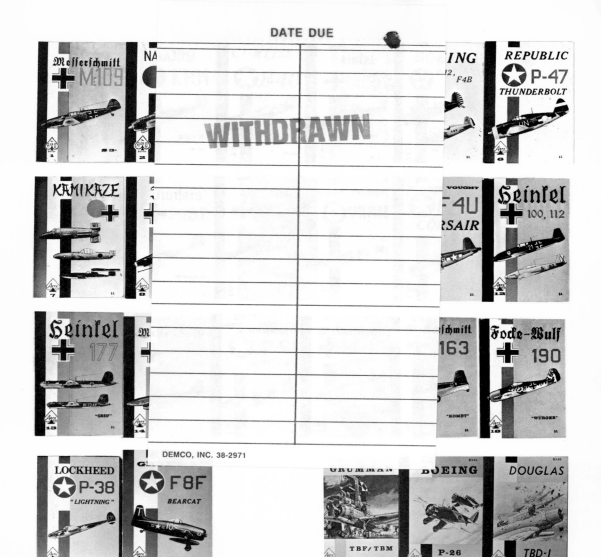

# AERO SERIES

A detailed look at many of the world's most famous and noteworthy military aircraft. Each book contains historical commentary, selected photographic material covering all aspects of the aircraft, technical data and specifications, four pages of color drawings, plus much more. Provides an unprecedented source of material for the modeler, military enthusiast, collector and historian. 52 7½ X 11 pages.

Volumes 1 thru 20 $3.00 (A) each.

ISBN-0-8168-0500-8   Vol. 1 MESSERSCHMITT ME 109
ISBN-0-8168-0504-0   Vol. 2 NAKAJIMA KI-84 (Frank)
ISBN-0-8168-0508-3   Vol. 3 The CURTISS P-40
ISBN-0-8168-0512-1   Vol. 4 The HEINKEL HE 162
ISBN-0-8168-0516-4   Vol. 5 BOEING P-12 F4b Fighter
ISBN-0-8168-0520-2   Vol. 6 REPUBLIC P-47
ISBN-0-8168-0524-5   Vol. 7 KAMIKAZE
ISBN-0-8168-0528-8   Vol. 8 JUNKERS JU-87 "Stuka"
ISBN-0-8168-0532-6   Vol. 9 DORNIER DO-335 "Pfeil"
ISBN-0-8168-0536-9   Vol. 10 SUPERMARINE SPITFIRE

ISBN-0-8168-0540-7   Vol. 11 CORSAIR Chance Vought F4U
ISBN-0-8168-0544-X   Vol. 12 HEINKEL 100, 112
ISBN-0-8168-0548-2   Vol. 13 HEINKEL HE 177 "Greif"
ISBN-0-8168-0552-0   Vol. 14 MESSERSCHMITT ME 262
ISBN-0-8168-0556-3   Vol. 15 MUSTANG North American P
ISBN-0-8168-0560-1   Vol. 16 MESSERSCHMITT Bf 110
ISBN-0-8168-0564-4   Vol. 17 MESSERSCHMITT ME 163
ISBN-0-8168-0568-7   Vol. 18 FOCKE WULF FW 190
ISBN-0-8168-0572-5   Vol. 19 LOCKHEED P-38
ISBN-0-8168-0576-8   Vol. 20 GRUMMAN F8F "Bearcat"

ISBN-0-8168-0580-6   Vol. 21, GRUMMAN TBF "Avenger"        $3.95(A)
ISBN-0-8168-0582-2   Vol. 21  GRUMMAN TBF SUPPLEMENT        $1.95(A)
ISBN-0-8168-0584-9   Vol. 22, BOEING P-26 "Pea-shooter"     $3.95(A)
ISBN-0-8168-0586-5   Vol. 23 DOUGLAS TBD-1 "Devastator"     $3.95(A)